HOW TO DIG A HOLE TO THE OTHER SIDE OF THE WORLD

by Faith McNulty

Pictures by Marc Simont

HarperTrophy
A Division of HarperCollins*Publishers*

How to Dig a Hole to the Other Side of the World
Text copyright © 1979 by Faith McNulty
Illustrations copyright © 1979 by Marc Simont
For information address HarperCollins
Children's Books, a division of HarperCollins
Publishers, 10 East 53rd Street, New York, NY 10022.

Library of Congress Cataloging-in-Publication Data
McNulty, Faith.
    How to dig a hole to the other side of the world.

    Summary: A child takes an imaginary 8,000-mile
journey through the earth and discovers what's inside.
    1. Earth—Internal structure—Juvenile literature.
[1. Earth—Internal structure]   I. Simont, Marc.
II. Title.
QE509.M244   1979   551.1'1   78-22479
ISBN 0-06-024147-0
ISBN 0-06-024148-9 (lib. bdg.)

To Richard

Find a soft place.
Take a shovel
and start to dig a hole.
The dirt you dig up is called loam.
Loam, or topsoil, is made up of
tiny bits of rock
mixed with many other things,
such as plants and worms that died
and rotted long ago.
When you have dug through the topsoil
you will come to clay or gravel or sand.
The digging will be harder.
When the hole is five or six feet deep,
you had better ask a friend to help.
He can pull up the clay or gravel
in a bucket,
while you stay at the bottom of the hole
and keep digging.

Sooner or later you will come to rocks;
all sorts of rocks; big rocks, little rocks;
granite, limestone, sandstone.
If you started your hole in Africa
you might find diamonds.
In Brazil you might find emeralds.
In other places you might find coal—
or gold or silver.
Wherever you dig watch for
old bones and shells.
The bones of many animals—
dinosaurs, giant tigers, turtles,
and other creatures of long ago—
are buried everywhere.
If you find some, dust them off carefully
and save them.

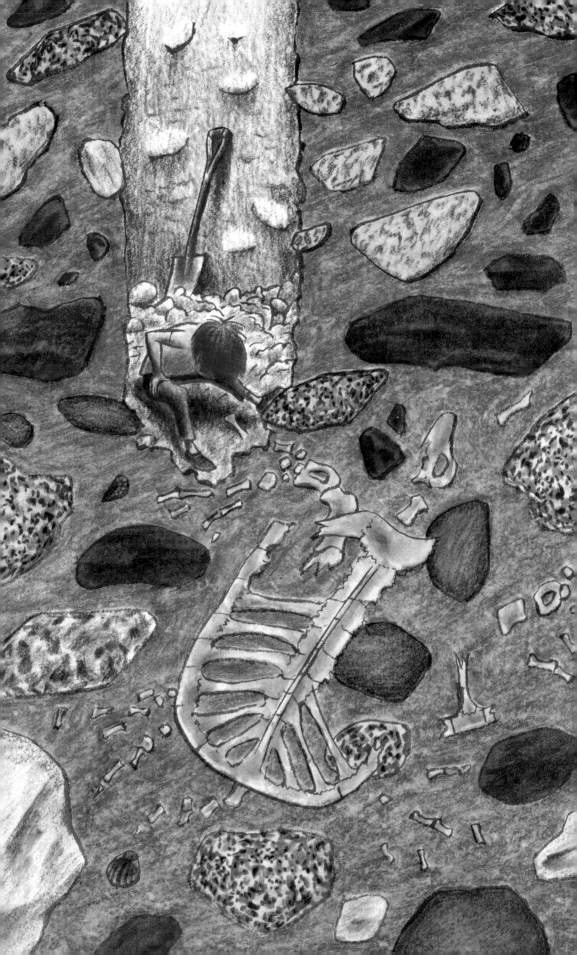

When you have dug about fifty feet down—
maybe more or maybe less—
you will come to solid rock.
This is the rocky skin of the earth,
called the crust. It is mostly granite.
To dig through it you will need
a drilling machine.
Start drilling.
You may hit water.
Rain sinks through the topsoil
and gathers in pools
and underground rivers.

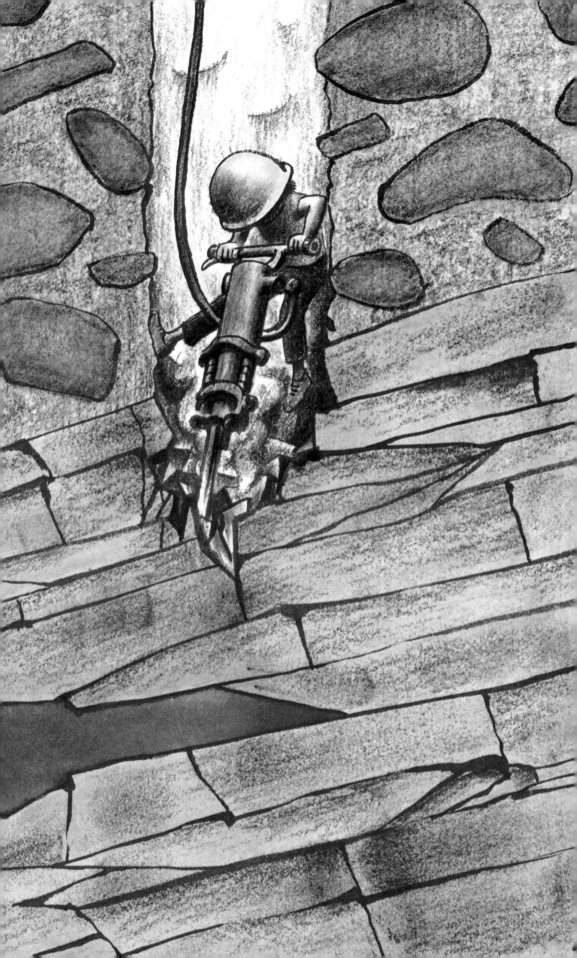

If you come to water you should put on
a diving suit.
You may come to a lake of black, gooey oil.
If you hit oil it would be best
to give up this hole and start another
somewhere else.

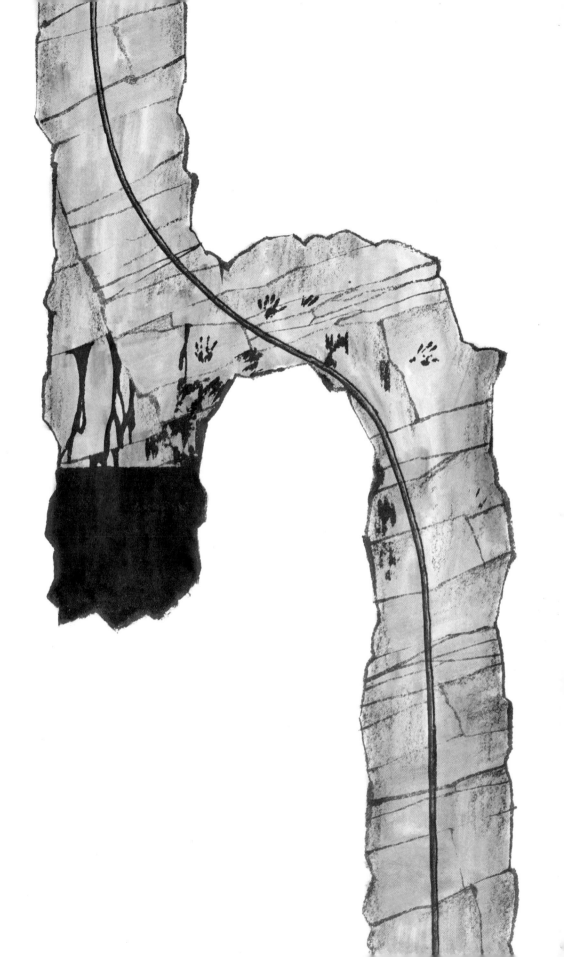

Keep drilling.
When you have drilled down a mile
or so, the rock will be warm.
This is because heat flows up into the rock
from the center of the earth.
You may hit boiling water or steam.
This is because rainwater drips down
through cracks onto very hot rock.
Sometimes it comes up again.
In some places on earth, hot water
bubbles up in springs,
or shoots up in geysers.
Because of the boiling water and steam
you will need an asbestos diving suit.
Stay out of the way of geysers.

If you got caught in a geyser it might
carry you up to the surface and shoot you
into the air. When you came down,
you would have to start digging all over again.
Keep drilling for ten or twenty miles.
You will come to a kind of rock called basalt.
Basalt is black and hard
and smooth and heavy.
There is a layer of basalt two or three miles
thick wrapped around the earth.
Keep drilling.
As you go deeper the basalt will get
hotter and hotter.
It will get so hot that it will melt
and glow dark red.
Melted basalt is called magma.

This is the stuff that sometimes
shoots out of cracks in the earth
and makes volcanoes. When it cools
on top of the ground, it is called lava.
Volcanoes are very dangerous.
Be careful and don't get caught in one.

To go through red-hot magma you will need
a jet-propelled submarine.
It must have a super
cooling system,
a fireproof skin and a drill
at the tip of its nose.
Your no-spaceship must be very strong.
An ordinary one would be squashed by the
weight of the magma around it.
Or burned up by the heat.
Down here below the crust of the earth
it is hotter than any fire you ever felt.
And it will get hotter and hotter
the deeper you go.
When you have gone down about
a hundred and fifty miles,
you are in what is called
the mantle of the earth.

NO-SPACESHIP

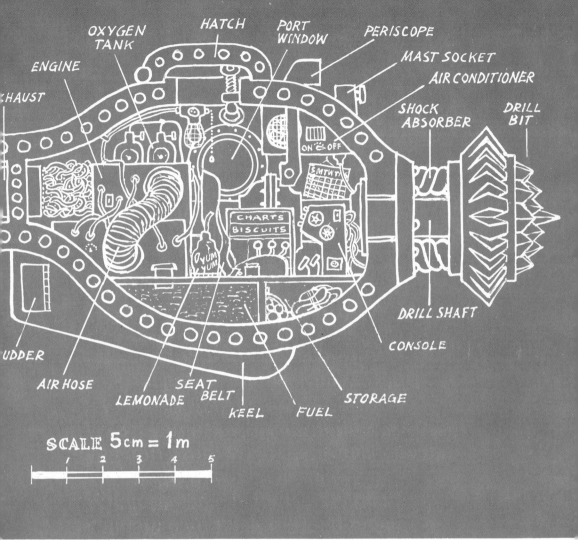

OXYGEN TANK
HATCH
PORT WINDOW
PERISCOPE
ENGINE
MAST SOCKET
AIR CONDITIONER
EXHAUST
SHOCK ABSORBER
DRILL BIT
ON & OFF
S M T W T
CHARTS
BISCUITS
YUM YUM
DRILL SHAFT
RUDDER
CONSOLE
AIR HOSE
SEAT BELT
LEMONADE
KEEL
FUEL
STORAGE

SCALE 5cm = 1m

1 2 3 4 5

The mantle is made of basalt that
is melted into goo and at the same
time is harder than steel.
It is melted by the great heat
and is hard because of the great weight above
pressing it down.

Keep drilling.
You still have a long way to go.
The mantle is 1700 miles thick.
As you go down, down, down,
in your fireproof submarine
you will notice that the color
of the mantle turns from red
to orange to yellow.

This is because it is getting
hotter and hotter.
At the bottom of the mantle
the temperature is more than
3000° Celsius.
It is so hot that if your ship caught fire
it wouldn't even leave an ash.
At the bottom of the mantle
you are more than halfway
to the center of the earth.

Now you must go through what is
called the outer core of the earth.
It is a mixture of melted rock and iron.
It is 1300 miles thick.
It will be hard going, but if you
have come this far you should keep on.
You are getting very close
to the center of the earth.
After the outer core comes the inner core.
The inner core of the earth is a ball
of solid iron.
It is so hot it glows
with white light.
Go 860 miles
straight down
and you will be at the center of the earth.

The center of the earth
is a place where
east meets west,
north meets south,
and up meets down.
At the center of the earth
there is nothing under you.
Every direction is up.
Your feet are pointing up
and your head is pointing up,
both at the same time.
Because there is nothing under you,
you will weigh nothing.
You will float inside your no-spaceship.

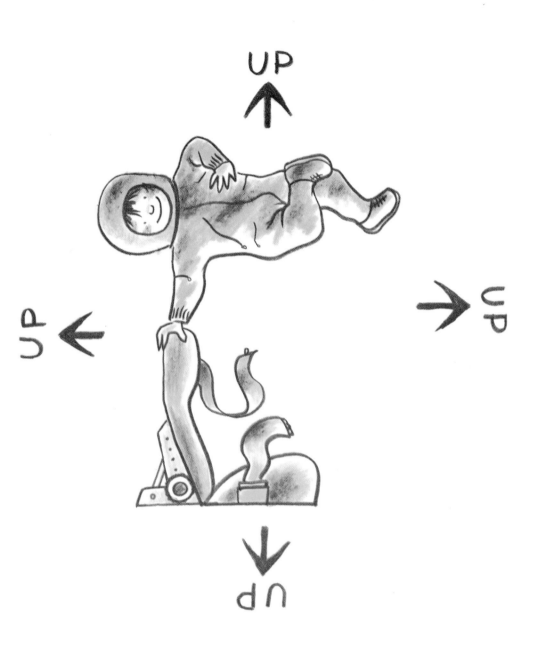

The weight of the whole world
will press down on your ship.
Do not stay long.
Go straight ahead and begin
the long trip up.

Go 860 miles
through the inner core
and 1300 miles through
the outer core.
Drill up and up through the mantle.
And then through the magma,
and then through the crust,
and then through rocks
and sand and clay.
At last you will come to the surface.
You will be about 8000 miles
from where you started to dig
on the opposite side of the world.
If you started in the United States
you will come up at the bottom of the
Indian Ocean.

It will be delightfully cool,
but full of sharks.
Stay in your submarine
and steer it to the top.
There you can open the hatch.
You will see the sky and the sun.
Or perhaps it will be night
and you will see the moon and the stars.
If you have a sail
hoist it and start sailing home.
Or else paddle.

When you get home you can
tell everyone
you have dug the deepest hole
in the world
and are very, very glad
to be back on top of the earth.

DATE			